JoJo Levesque Unstoppable

A Story of Fame, Struggles, and Triumph

JAMES B. WHITE

Copyright

Disclaimer

This book is an independent, unauthorized biography and is not affiliated with or endorsed by JoJo Levesque, her management, or any associated entities. It is intended to provide readers with an insightful exploration of JoJo's career and life journey, based on publicly available information, interviews, and research. The content reflects the author's perspectives and interpretations and is presented with respect to JoJo Levesque's personal and professional story.

Table of Contents

Introduction

In the ever-shifting world of the entertainment industry, few stories capture both the intense pressures and the powerful resilience it demands quite like JoJo Levesque's journey. From her meteoric rise as a young pop sensation to facing unexpected challenges that put her career on hold, JoJo's life has been a testament to the highs and lows of fame, struggle, and unbreakable spirit.

"JoJo Levesque Unstoppable: A Story of Fame, Struggles, and Triumph" goes beyond the spotlight, delving into the complex path JoJo has walked from an early age. With a talent that captivated audiences worldwide, JoJo seemed

destined for an unstoppable ascent, yet her journey was punctuated by battles with record labels, personal struggles, and a fight for her voice—both figuratively and literally. In an industry that often seems designed to silence rather than uplift, JoJo's tenacity shines as a beacon of courage and self-discovery.

This book offers a window into her determination and resilience, exploring the defining moments that led JoJo not only back to the stage but to a place of creative and personal freedom. It's the story of an artist who never let setbacks dictate her future, carving her own path with fierce authenticity and inspiring countless fans along the way.

Prepare to follow JoJo Levesque on a compelling journey—a tale of grit, passion, and, ultimately, triumph over adversity.

Chapter One

A Star is Born

Joanna Noëlle Levesque, known to the world as JoJo, was born on December 20, 1990, in Brattleboro, Vermont, into a family deeply rooted in music. Raised primarily by her mother after her parents divorced when she was only four years old, JoJo's journey into the entertainment world started early. From a young age, she was surrounded by the sounds of soul, gospel, and R&B, which were staples in her household. Her mother, Diana Levesque, a classically trained singer, would practice hymns and musical theater pieces, inspiring JoJo to follow suit. By the age of two, JoJo was already imitating songs and melodies, signaling the beginning of her incredible talent.

Growing up in Foxborough, Massachusetts, JoJo's early years were characterized by humble beginnings. Despite financial struggles and the challenge of being raised by a single mother, JoJo's raw talent and dedication set her apart. Her mother recognized her gift early on and encouraged her to perform at local talent shows and competitions, where JoJo's powerhouse vocals became the talk of the town. While most kids her age were playing with toys or spending time outdoors, JoJo was busy perfecting her craft, imitating legends like Whitney Houston, Etta James, and Aretha Franklin, whose soul-infused vocal styles would greatly influence her own.

JoJo's big break came at the age of six when she appeared on the television show *Kids Say the Darndest Things* hosted by Bill Cosby. She sang a rendition of Cher's "If I Could Turn Back Time," stunning the audience and the host with her powerful voice. This exposure led to a series of television appearances, including a stint on the talent show *America's Most Talented Kids*, where she showcased her vocal prowess by covering Aretha Franklin's "Respect" and "Chain of Fools." Though JoJo did not win the competition, her performance caught the attention of record producer Vincent Herbert, who was so impressed that he invited her to audition for Blackground Records.

At just 12 years old, JoJo signed a major recording deal with Blackground Records. The youngest artist ever to sign with the label, JoJo soon began working with top producers on her debut album. Her breakout moment came in 2004 when she released the single "Leave (Get Out)" at the age of 13. The song's infectious melody and mature lyrical content resonated with listeners, and it quickly climbed to the top of the Billboard charts. JoJo made history as the youngest solo artist to have a debut single reach number one on the Billboard Mainstream Top 40, a feat that solidified her status as a pop sensation. Her success with "Leave (Get Out)" not only made her a household name but also opened doors for her to explore other areas of entertainment.

The release of JoJo's debut album *JoJo* later that year was met with widespread acclaim. The album, a blend of pop, R&B, and soul, showcased her impressive vocal range and emotional depth, particularly for someone so young. Songs like "Baby It's You" and "Not That Kinda Girl" demonstrated her versatility, cementing her place as a rising star in the music industry. The album went platinum, selling over 3 million copies worldwide, and marked the beginning of what appeared to be a long and fruitful career. JoJo's ability to connect with audiences, especially young listeners, was rooted in her relatability. She wasn't just a polished pop star; she was a young girl dealing with real emotions, and she wasn't afraid to express that through her music.

But JoJo's journey wasn't without challenges. Behind the scenes, her home life was fraught with difficulties. Her father, Joel Levesque, battled addiction, and the strain it placed on their relationship weighed heavily on JoJo. Despite this, her mother remained a constant source of strength and guidance. JoJo has often spoken about how her mother sacrificed everything to help her succeed, driving her to auditions and performances across the country while managing their financial hardships.

In many ways, JoJo's early career was both a blessing and a burden. While she achieved immense success at a young age, the pressures of fame, combined with her family's struggles, forced her to grow up quickly. Unlike many of her peers, JoJo didn't have the luxury of a carefree childhood. The expectations placed on her by the music industry and the responsibility she felt toward her family weighed heavily on her shoulders. Still, JoJo pushed forward, determined to make the most of the opportunities she had been given.

By the time she was 15, JoJo had not only conquered the music charts but had also begun making a name for herself in Hollywood. She starred in the 2006 film *Aquamarine*, playing a teenage girl who befriends a mermaid, and the family comedy *R.V.* alongside Robin Williams. JoJo's transition from singer to actress seemed seamless, and she was well on her way to becoming a multi-faceted star.

However, despite her meteoric rise, JoJo's early years in the spotlight were not without complications. As she navigated the music industry, she began to experience the darker side of fame. The pressure to maintain her image, the lack of creative control, and the grueling demands of touring took a toll on her mental and emotional well-being. Moreover, as a teenager in the public eye, JoJo often felt like she was under a microscope, scrutinized for her every move. This sense of being constantly watched and judged would later contribute to the struggles she faced as an adult.

Despite these challenges, JoJo's passion for music and her drive to succeed kept her moving forward. The resilience she displayed during these early years would serve as a foundation for the trials that lay ahead. As she matured, JoJo's ability to channel her personal experiences into her music only grew stronger, allowing her to create songs that resonated with listeners on a deeper level.

Chapter Two

Meteoric Rise to Fame

At just 13 years old, JoJo burst onto the music scene in a way few could have predicted. The release of her debut single "Leave (Get Out)" in 2004 not only catapulted her into stardom but also made her the youngest solo artist ever to top the Billboard Pop Songs chart. Her meteoric rise was swift, and it seemed the world had discovered a new teen sensation whose voice defied her young age. However, JoJo's story wasn't just about teenage success; it was about an artist with the vocal ability and emotional maturity far beyond her years, navigating the pressures of the entertainment industry while grappling with her own personal challenges.

JoJo's initial success was a result of both talent and timing. Growing up in a musical household, she was immersed in a wide array of genres, from R&B and soul to jazz, all of which would later influence her sound. Her mother, a singer trained in musical theater, played a significant role in nurturing her talent. JoJo began performing as early as six years old, appearing on TV shows like *America's Most Talented Kid* and *Kids Say the Darndest Things*, where her powerful voice stunned audiences and caught the attention of music executives. But it wasn't until record producer Vincent Herbert discovered her that the wheels were set in motion for what would become her career-defining debut.

Signing with Blackground Records at the age of 12, JoJo was immediately paired with some of the best producers and songwriters in the industry. The team crafted a sound that blended pop and R&B, perfectly suited to her voice, which had an emotional depth that belied her age. "Leave (Get Out)" became an anthem of youthful defiance, resonating with audiences both young and old. The song's catchy hook, coupled with JoJo's heartfelt delivery, made it a massive hit. It wasn't just the catchy melody, but the conviction in her voice that made listeners take notice. She wasn't just a young girl singing pop; she was a vocalist commanding attention, with lyrics that spoke to betrayal and heartbreak—universal themes that resonated deeply.

Her debut album, *JoJo*, released in June 2004, further solidified her place in the music world. It sold over 95,000 copies in its first week and eventually went platinum, showcasing JoJo's ability to draw in fans beyond just her breakout single. Tracks like "Baby It's You" and "Not That Kinda Girl" continued to build on her image as a strong, independent young artist. With her soulful voice and relatable lyrics, JoJo quickly gained a following, not just as a teen sensation but as a serious artist in the making.

As her music career flourished, JoJo also ventured into acting. In 2006, she starred in the teen comedy *Aquamarine* alongside Emma Roberts and Sara Paxton. The film, a lighthearted coming-of-age story, allowed JoJo to showcase her versatility as a performer. That same year, she also appeared in *RV* opposite Robin Williams, further proving that she wasn't just a one-trick pony. Her ability to balance both acting and singing while maintaining a strong presence in each industry was a testament to her work ethic and talent.

Behind the scenes, however, the pressure of fame was mounting. JoJo, while enjoying the fruits of her early success, was also grappling with the realities of being a teenage star. The music industry, known for its demanding nature, wasn't always kind to young artists. JoJo had to grow up quickly, navigating a world of adults, contractual obligations, and the ever-present scrutiny of the media. In interviews, she would later reflect on the difficulties of having her adolescence play out in the public eye, the pressure to conform to industry standards, and the challenges of maintaining authenticity in a world that often wanted to shape her into something she wasn't.

Despite these challenges, JoJo continued to push forward. Her sophomore album, *The High Road*, released in 2006, was another critical and commercial success. It featured the hit single "Too Little Too Late," which became one of her most iconic songs. The track's soaring vocals and emotive lyrics once again showcased JoJo's ability to tap into universal emotions of heartache and moving on. The song broke records, jumping from No. 66 to No. 3 on the Billboard Hot 100 in just one week—a testament to its widespread appeal.

However, while everything appeared to be going well on the surface, storm clouds were beginning to gather. Unbeknownst to the public, JoJo was becoming increasingly entangled in legal disputes with her record label, Blackground Records. The label, which had helped launch her career, began to experience financial difficulties, and JoJo found herself caught in the crossfire. Over the next several years, her third studio album was delayed multiple times, and despite her desire to release new music, she was legally bound by a contract that wouldn't allow it. As a result, JoJo's once-thriving career seemed to be at a standstill, leaving her frustrated and unsure of what the future held.

But even during these difficult years, JoJo didn't disappear completely. She continued to tour, released mixtapes independently, and maintained a close connection with her fans. Despite the legal battles and professional setbacks, she remained committed to her craft, waiting for the day when she could regain control of her music and her career.

JoJo's meteoric rise in the mid-2000s wasn't just a flash in the pan; it was the beginning of a long, complex journey that would see her face more challenges than most artists experience in a lifetime. Her voice, which had carried her to the top of the charts as a teenager, remained her greatest asset. But as she would later prove, it was her resilience and determination that truly set her apart. What could have been a typical teen star story, filled with early success followed by obscurity, instead became a tale of perseverance, survival, and an eventual fierce comeback that would define her legacy in the music industry.

Chapter Three

The Hollywood Dream

Joanna "JoJo" Levesque was not just a teen pop sensation; she was an artist with undeniable talent, ready to take on the world at a young age. However, as JoJo began her ascent in the music industry, Hollywood took notice of the multi-talented star, and her transition to acting began to unfold. The early 2000s were a defining time for JoJo as she balanced her skyrocketing music career with her aspirations in film, a challenge that many young artists often face. This chapter of her life reflects her versatility as a performer, her drive to expand her horizons, and the challenges of juggling fame at such a young age.

JoJo's first major foray into acting came in 2006 when she starred in the film *Aquamarine*, a family-friendly fantasy comedy. In the movie, she played Hailey, one of two best friends who discover a mermaid. Alongside her co-stars, Emma Roberts and Sara Paxton, JoJo showcased a natural charm on screen. *Aquamarine* became a popular film among young audiences, and JoJo's role was pivotal to its appeal. It was her ability to seamlessly step into the world of acting that signaled to critics and fans alike that JoJo was more than just a pop star.

This wasn't her only venture into acting that year. JoJo also starred opposite the legendary Robin Williams in *R.V.*, a family comedy that allowed her to further demonstrate her acting range. In the film, JoJo played Cassie Munro, the teenage daughter of a man trying to reconnect with his family on a disastrous road trip. Acting alongside an iconic comedian like Williams was no small feat, but JoJo held her own, adding a fresh and relatable teenage perspective to the comedy. The role gave her a chance to step out of the pop-star persona and show a different side of herself, which she did with grace and ease. These two films put JoJo in the spotlight as an actress, opening doors for future opportunities.

However, as much as her acting career was starting to take off, JoJo was still at the center of her musical career, touring and promoting her records. By this time, she had already released her second album, *The High Road*, in 2006, which included the smash hit "Too Little Too Late." The success of her music was undeniable, but her growing acting career demanded her attention too. For JoJo, balancing these two worlds was no easy task. She often spoke about the difficulties of managing both music and acting commitments, but it was clear that she was determined to prove herself in both arenas.

Hollywood can be an enticing yet demanding industry, especially for young stars. JoJo, with her fame at its peak, found herself navigating an industry that is known for being unforgiving, particularly to women and young artists. The pressures of maintaining a pristine image, staying relevant in music, and proving her worth in acting undoubtedly took a toll on her. Hollywood, after all, can be a double-edged sword—while it offers opportunities, it also presents challenges that can easily derail a career. For JoJo, the challenge was not just to sustain success, but also to stay true to herself amid the industry's demands.

JoJo's acting roles helped cement her status as a household name, but the experience also revealed some of the complexities of fame. In an industry where image is often everything, JoJo faced the pressures of being a teenage girl under constant scrutiny. Hollywood was also evolving, with the rise of social media and tabloids making it even harder for young stars to maintain privacy. For JoJo, this meant dealing with constant speculation about her personal life, her relationships, and even her physical appearance.

In interviews, JoJo would later reflect on how these pressures contributed to her struggles with body image and self-esteem. The pressure to conform to a particular Hollywood standard of beauty left her feeling insecure, even as she was winning accolades for her music and acting. As JoJo's star continued to rise, so did the internal conflicts she faced as a young woman trying to find her place in an industry that often commodified youth and appearance.

It wasn't long before JoJo's music career started facing hurdles as well. Issues with her record label, Blackground Records, began to emerge, and they significantly impacted both her acting and music career. The label put her music on hold, preventing her from releasing new material. This legal entanglement would lead to a years-long hiatus from mainstream music, but it also meant that JoJo's acting career took a backseat. She found herself in limbo, unable to release the music she loved and without the consistent acting roles that could keep her in the spotlight. Hollywood's allure had dimmed for JoJo as she focused on fighting for her freedom in the music industry.

Despite these setbacks, JoJo's talent remained undeniable. Hollywood may have momentarily taken a step back from the young star, but she continued to persevere. While her film roles in the late 2000s and early 2010s were fewer, JoJo never lost sight of her dream to return to both music and acting. She dabbled in smaller projects, including appearances in TV shows like *Hawaii Five-0* and *Lethal Weapon*. These appearances, while brief, were a reminder of JoJo's enduring appeal as an actress. She had not abandoned Hollywood; she was simply biding her time.

As JoJo's story unfolded, it became clear that the Hollywood dream, while appealing, was never going to define her entirely. She was an artist, first and foremost, who happened to have a talent for acting. But as the 2010s progressed, her focus began to shift back to music, the true passion that had sparked her career in the first place. JoJo's fierce comeback, both in music and in life, would ultimately define this period of her journey.

Chapter Four

Label Struggles and Career Pause

JoJo Levesque, known for her powerful voice and meteoric rise to fame as a teenager, faced an obstacle that many fans were unaware of during her early years in the spotlight. While her debut single "Leave (Get Out)" and subsequent album *The High Road* cemented her status as a pop and R&B sensation, behind the scenes, JoJo was dealing with a significant struggle that brought her flourishing career to a grinding halt. Her battle with her record label, Blackground Records, became a defining moment in her life—a period marked by frustration, legal entanglements, and the fight to regain control over her own career. This tumultuous chapter not only stalled her career but also nearly derailed her passion for music.

JoJo signed her first record deal with Blackground Records at just 12 years old. As a young artist, she relied heavily on the guidance of her label to navigate the complexities of the music industry. Initially, Blackground Records provided her with the resources and support she needed to achieve success, and her debut album, *JoJo* (2004), was a commercial hit. At only 13 years old, she became the youngest solo artist to have a number one single on the Billboard Mainstream Top 40 chart. Her voice, mature beyond her years, drew comparisons to established R&B stars, and her future seemed bound for even greater heights.

However, after the release of her second album *The High Road* in 2006, JoJo's career trajectory began to shift in ways she hadn't anticipated. Despite her growing fanbase and consistent chart success, Blackground Records inexplicably delayed the release of her third album. JoJo had already recorded new music and was eager to continue her rise in the industry, but Blackground's internal issues—reportedly due to financial difficulties and mismanagement—left her music in limbo. As a result, years passed without any new releases, leaving JoJo's fans confused and frustrated.

What many didn't know at the time was that JoJo was effectively trapped in her contract with Blackground Records. She was bound by a deal that restricted her ability to release new music without the label's approval, and Blackground wasn't budging. JoJo found herself in a legal battle, fighting for the freedom to release the music she had poured her heart into. The label's refusal to allow her to move forward stifled her creativity and made it impossible for her to fulfill the promises she had made to her fans and herself.

During this career pause, JoJo continued to write and record music, but much of it remained unheard. She released two mixtapes independently—*Can't Take That Away from Me* (2010) and *Agápē* (2012)—as a way to stay connected with her audience. These projects were not only a creative outlet for JoJo but also a form of rebellion against the restrictions placed on her. Still, the reality of being sidelined by her label took a toll on her mental and emotional well-being. The frustration of having her art suppressed, coupled with the pressure of maintaining a public image, pushed her to the brink of despair.

In interviews, JoJo has spoken candidly about this dark period in her life. She described how the industry's rejection of her music left her feeling abandoned and doubting her own worth as an artist. She also revealed the strain that the ongoing legal battle with Blackground Records had on her personal life. At a time when she should have been thriving, JoJo was fighting just to be heard.

The legal battle between JoJo and Blackground Records lasted for nearly a decade. As the years passed, the once-unstoppable young star was seen less frequently in the media, and many wondered what had happened to her promising career. The industry had moved on, and JoJo was left watching from the sidelines as her peers continued to release music and dominate the charts. The delay in her career caused her to miss out on key years of artistic development and growth, which are crucial for any young musician.

Despite these setbacks, JoJo's resilience never wavered. In 2013, she filed a lawsuit against Blackground Records, seeking to be released from her contract on the grounds that she had been legally bound to the label since she was a minor, and therefore the contract was no longer valid. The court ruled in her favor, finally freeing JoJo from the shackles of her restrictive deal. After nearly a decade of fighting, JoJo was liberated, and she immediately began working on her comeback.

In 2014, JoJo signed with Atlantic Records, marking the beginning of a new chapter in her career. The years of struggle had only deepened her passion for music, and her return to the studio felt like a long-overdue homecoming. In 2016, she released her third studio album, *Mad Love*, a deeply personal project that showcased her growth as an artist and a person. The album was well-received, and JoJo's comeback was hailed as one of the most triumphant in the music industry.

Even after winning her legal battle, JoJo faced another challenge: reclaiming her music. Due to the contract with Blackground Records, her first two albums were unavailable on streaming platforms for years. JoJo took matters into her own hands once again and re-recorded both her debut album *JoJo* and *The High Road* in 2018 under her own label, Clover Music. These re-releases allowed her to regain control of her early work, a symbolic act of taking back what was rightfully hers.

JoJo's battle with her record label is a cautionary tale of the pitfalls young artists can face when entering the industry. But it is also a story of triumph. JoJo's ability to persevere through years of legal struggles and emerge stronger speaks to her unbreakable spirit. Her journey is a testament to the importance of owning one's voice and refusing to be silenced, no matter the obstacles.

Chapter Five

Personal Struggles

JoJo Levesque's path to success seemed straight out of a Hollywood dream. She had the voice, the charisma, and the world at her feet at just 13. However, behind the glittering public image of a teen pop sensation lay a storm of personal struggles, one that would challenge her strength and force her to confront demons rooted in her past.

Born into a home marked by addiction and mental health issues, JoJo's earliest memories were shaped by chaos. Her father, Joel Levesque, battled addiction for most of his life. He was a talented man, a singer who performed for fun, but addiction ultimately stole that joy from him. Her mother, Diana, was her constant—raising JoJo as a single parent after her parents' divorce when JoJo was just four years old. Diana was musically inclined as well, singing in a Catholic church choir and performing in musical theater. JoJo's connection to music was undeniably linked to her mother's influence, but the darker side of her upbringing loomed large.

Growing up, JoJo found herself navigating an environment where addiction was a constant presence. Despite these struggles, music provided her with an escape. From a young age, she was driven, and by the time she reached her teens, she was already a star. Her debut single, **"Leave (Get Out),"** was a massive success, making her the youngest solo artist to top the Billboard Mainstream Top 40 chart. But behind the scenes, the pressure of being thrust into fame at such a young age weighed heavily on her. She was balancing her childhood, family instability, and a rapidly rising career, with little room to process her emotions.

By the time JoJo hit her late teens, her career took an unexpected turn. Her record label, Blackground Records, became the source of immense frustration and professional stagnation. Despite her desire to release new music and continue her momentum, the label shelved her third studio album for years, refusing to allow her to release new material. This contractual entanglement, which lasted nearly a decade, was more than a professional setback—it was personal devastation. JoJo, who had built her identity around music, was left powerless, her voice silenced by corporate control.

During this dark period, JoJo turned to unhealthy coping mechanisms. She has candidly shared that she used alcohol to numb the pain of feeling abandoned by the industry that had once celebrated her. In interviews, JoJo described this time as one of deep despair, recounting how she would drink excessively in an attempt to escape her reality. She recalls hitting rock bottom, waking up one day and realizing that she was in a destructive cycle, much like the one she had witnessed in her father. It was a moment of painful clarity—she was walking the same path of addiction that had haunted her family for generations.

JoJo's struggles didn't stop with addiction. As a young woman in the public eye, she faced intense scrutiny over her appearance. The entertainment industry's unforgiving standards took a toll on her self-esteem. JoJo revealed in later years that she had turned to extreme measures to lose weight during her career's downtime. She resorted to injections and fad diets, desperate to conform to the industry's beauty ideals. The pressure to look a certain way compounded her feelings of inadequacy, leading her to question her self-worth. She described feeling out of control of her own life—her music was held hostage, her body scrutinized, and her self-image shattered.

However, despite the overwhelming challenges she faced, JoJo was determined to regain control of her life. She made the difficult decision to enter therapy, focusing on her mental health and well-being. It wasn't an easy journey, but JoJo's resilience shone through. Therapy helped her confront the unresolved trauma from her childhood and the unhealthy coping mechanisms she had developed. She began to understand the importance of self-love and acceptance, learning to break the cycle of addiction that had plagued her family.

One of the turning points in JoJo's recovery came when she decided to re-record her early albums. This decision was more than just a business move—it was symbolic of JoJo reclaiming her voice and her autonomy. By re-recording her albums, *JoJo* and *The High Road*, JoJo was sending a message: she would no longer allow the music industry to control her narrative. The re-recordings, released under her own label, Clover Music, marked the beginning of a new chapter in her life—one where she was in charge.

JoJo's comeback wasn't just about music; it was about healing. She found herself in a place of self-acceptance, recognizing that her struggles had made her stronger. In interviews, JoJo spoke about how her experiences with addiction, self-doubt, and body image had shaped her into the person she is today. She no longer sees these struggles as weaknesses but as part of her journey toward resilience. JoJo's decision to be open about her personal battles has resonated with many, making her not just an artist, but a symbol of strength for those who have faced similar struggles.

Today, JoJo continues to use her platform to inspire others. She has embraced her imperfections, sharing her story with the world in the hopes of helping others who may be going through similar challenges. JoJo's journey is a testament to the power of resilience, the importance of self-love, and the strength it takes to rebuild one's life after hitting rock bottom.

Chapter Six

Fierce Comeback

JoJo's story of resilience and fierce comeback is nothing short of inspirational. After years of legal battles and personal struggles, she demonstrated a tenacity that few artists ever have to summon. Her rise back to the top, after years in the industry wilderness, speaks to her unwavering belief in herself and her ability to defy the odds.

JoJo first burst onto the scene in 2004 as a 13-year-old sensation with her hit single "Leave (Get Out)," which not only topped the charts but also made her the youngest solo artist ever to score a number-one single in the U.S. Despite her early success, JoJo's career was plagued by contractual issues with her label, Blackground Records, which essentially stalled her progress for nearly a decade. During this time, she wasn't able to release any new albums, despite her desire to continue sharing her music with the world. As she grew older, she watched her peers in the music industry continue to thrive while she fought a legal battle that kept her sidelined.

For an artist like JoJo, whose passion for music had been her driving force since childhood, this was more than just a career roadblock; it was a deeply personal struggle. JoJo felt trapped by the very industry she had once dominated. The legal dispute revolved around her contract with Blackground Records, which had effectively frozen her ability to release new music or sign with another label. This not only hampered her creativity but also took a serious toll on her mental health. She described feeling as if she had been stripped of her identity, as music was the core of who she was. During this time, JoJo turned to songwriting as a form of therapy, releasing mixtapes like *Can't Take That Away from Me* (2010) and *Agápē* (2012) as a way to stay connected to her fans and keep her artistry alive, even though she was unable to officially release studio albums.

In 2013, after a lengthy legal battle, JoJo finally won her freedom from her contract with Blackground Records. This victory was monumental, not only for JoJo but also for other artists who have found themselves in similar legal struggles with their labels. Free at last from the legal shackles that had bound her for so long, JoJo wasted no time in getting back to work. In 2014, she signed with Atlantic Records, a major step forward in reclaiming her career. This partnership allowed JoJo to release her long-awaited third studio album, *Mad Love*, in 2016.

Mad Love was more than just a comeback album; it was a statement of JoJo's resilience and growth as both an artist and a woman. The album, which debuted at number six on the Billboard 200, was a mix of pop, R&B, and soul that showcased her powerful vocals and emotional depth. The lead single, "Fuck Apologies," featuring Wiz Khalifa, was emblematic of JoJo's new attitude—unapologetic, bold, and completely in control of her narrative. This album marked her return to the industry, but it was also a testament to how much she had grown personally. Songs like "I Am" and "Honest" were deeply reflective, speaking to her experiences of self-doubt and the eventual rediscovery of her worth.

Even though *Mad Love* was a critical and commercial success, JoJo's journey wasn't over. She knew that reclaiming her career meant more than just releasing one album—it was about owning her art. This realization led to an even more profound chapter in her story: re-recording her early albums. In 2018, JoJo re-recorded her first two albums, *JoJo* and *The High Road*, under her own label, Clover Music, which she founded after leaving Atlantic Records. This decision wasn't just about regaining control of her music; it was also about ensuring that her early work, which had defined her as an artist, was available to fans on streaming platforms. Due to the legal dispute with Blackground

Records, her original albums had been pulled from digital platforms, making them inaccessible to a generation of listeners. By re-recording these albums, JoJo not only gave fans a chance to reconnect with her early music but also demonstrated the importance of artists having control over their work.

This era also saw JoJo dive deeper into advocacy, especially around mental health. She became more vocal about her own struggles with body image, addiction, and self-worth, sharing her journey with her fans in a way that was both candid and empowering. She discussed how, during the years when her career was stalled, she struggled with depression and turned to unhealthy coping mechanisms to deal with the pressure. Her openness about these struggles helped break down the stigma surrounding mental health in the music industry, where the pressures of fame can often be overwhelming.

JoJo's comeback was not just about re-establishing her presence in the music industry; it was about reclaiming her identity and redefining what success meant to her. By taking control of her narrative and refusing to be defined by the setbacks she had faced, JoJo emerged not just as a pop star but as a resilient and empowered artist. Her story is a testament to the power of perseverance, self-belief, and the importance of fighting for one's art.

Today, JoJo continues to push boundaries in her career, exploring new musical styles and expanding her artistry. In 2023, she made her Broadway debut in *Moulin Rouge! The Musical*, further showcasing her versatility as a performer.

With her own label, new music on the way, and a dedicated fanbase behind her, JoJo has proven that she is unbreakable, not just as an artist but as a woman who has triumphed over adversity.

Chapter Seven

A Star Reborn

After years of facing legal battles, industry hurdles, and personal struggles, JoJo Levesque made one of the most powerful comebacks in entertainment history. Her story of resilience is encapsulated in her return not only to music but also her newfound success on the stage of Broadway. The young star who had burst onto the scene at age 13 with her chart-topping single **"Leave (Get Out)"** found herself in the spotlight once again, but this time, it was different. JoJo was not just the teenage pop sensation that audiences once knew; she had transformed into a seasoned artist with a deeper understanding of her craft and herself.

JoJo's journey back to fame was not a simple one. After a tumultuous period where she was tied down by restrictive contracts and silenced by the music industry, JoJo had to fight her way out of a legal labyrinth to reclaim her right to release music. Her victory was hard-won, but it marked the beginning of a new chapter, one where she was in control of her career. She took bold steps by re-recording and re-releasing her first two albums under her own label, Clover Music, a move that symbolized her newfound independence and determination to take back what was rightfully hers. These albums, *JoJo* and *The High Road*, represented more than just music; they were the embodiment of a fight for artistic freedom.

But JoJo's resilience went beyond the recording studio. In 2023, she made her Broadway debut in

Moulin Rouge! The Musical, stepping into the role of Satine. It was a role that required not only vocal prowess but a deep emotional range, and JoJo delivered on both fronts. Her performance was met with critical acclaim, with audiences praising her ability to bring vulnerability and strength to the character. This was not just a return to the stage but a reinvention of JoJo as an artist who could transcend the boundaries of pop music and step into the world of live theatre with grace and power. It was a moment that solidified her transformation from a former child star into a mature, multifaceted performer.

The decision to join *Moulin Rouge!* was a bold one, but it came at a time when JoJo was ready to push the boundaries of her career. After spending years in the shadows, restricted by her record label, Broadway offered her the chance to explore a new form of expression. Stepping onto the Broadway stage required JoJo to challenge herself in ways she had never done before. It was no longer about perfecting a radio hit or maintaining a public image as a pop star—it was about embodying a character and connecting with an audience in real-time. The immersive nature of theatre allowed JoJo to bring her authentic self to the role, blending her personal experiences with the narrative of the show.

Her portrayal of Satine came at a pivotal moment in her career, one where JoJo was embracing her past struggles and transforming them into sources of strength. In interviews, JoJo reflected on how her own life experiences—ranging from her early fame, her struggles with addiction, and the loss of her father—gave her a deeper connection to the character of Satine, a courtesan fighting for survival in the bohemian world of Paris. JoJo's life had been a fight for survival in many ways, both in the music industry and in her personal battles. This made her performance on stage even more compelling, as it was infused with real emotions and raw vulnerability.

Critics noted that JoJo's voice, which had always been her signature asset, took on a new depth and maturity in the role of Satine. While she had always been known for her powerful vocals, the emotional weight behind her singing was undeniable in her Broadway performances. Songs like *"Come What May"* took on new meaning when sung by JoJo, as she channeled the intensity of her own journey into the music. It was clear to everyone watching that JoJo had grown not just as a singer but as an artist capable of conveying complex emotions through her voice and her stage presence.

JoJo's success on Broadway was not just a personal victory—it was a reminder to her fans and the entertainment industry of her undeniable talent and resilience. She had been written off by many during her years of absence from the music scene, but her comeback was proof that true talent could not be silenced. JoJo had fought against the odds, battled through personal demons, and emerged stronger than ever. Her time on Broadway was a testament to her ability to adapt, evolve, and continue pushing the boundaries of her career.

The significance of her Broadway debut cannot be overstated. For JoJo, this was not just another career milestone but a symbolic rebirth. After years of feeling stifled by the music industry, Broadway offered her a platform to showcase her talent in a new way and on her terms. It was a space where she could be vulnerable, open, and authentic, and her fans responded to that authenticity. Many who had grown up listening to JoJo's early hits felt a renewed connection to her as she embarked on this new chapter of her career.

In many ways, JoJo's journey mirrors that of the character she played on stage. Both Satine and JoJo faced immense challenges and fought for their place in the world. Just as Satine defied the odds in *Moulin Rouge!*, JoJo defied the industry that had tried to hold her back. Her story is one of unbreakable spirit, fierce determination, and the courage to keep moving forward, even when the path seemed impossible.

Chapter Eight

Legacy of Resilience

JoJo Levesque's story is a testament to resilience, a journey marked by remarkable highs and devastating lows, only to emerge stronger and more self-assured than ever. At the height of her fame in the mid-2000s, JoJo was a household name, known for her powerhouse vocals and relatable lyrics that connected with young listeners across the globe. However, behind the scenes, her battle with a stifling record contract and personal struggles nearly silenced her. Yet, what sets JoJo apart is her ability to turn pain into fuel, rising from the ashes of an unjust industry and personal turmoil to reclaim her voice and redefine her legacy.

For many artists, the industry can be an unforgiving place, and for JoJo, it was no different. Signed to a major record label at just 12 years old, she became a pop sensation almost overnight. Her debut single, "Leave (Get Out)," dominated the charts, making her the youngest solo artist to top the Billboard charts in the U.S. She followed up her success with *The High Road* and the hit single "Too Little Too Late," proving that she was no one-hit-wonder. Yet, beneath the glitz and glamour, JoJo faced a battle that would nearly strip her of her career.

Her label, Blackground Records, put a halt to her music, refusing to release new material or allow her to explore other opportunities. For years, JoJo was locked in a legal and emotional straitjacket, unable to share her talent with the world. The frustration and helplessness of this period were palpable; a young artist, full of potential and creativity, was being stifled at the hands of corporate greed. JoJo was vocal about how this standoff with her label took a toll on her mental health, even leading her to question her worth as an artist and individual. It was during this period that JoJo began to unravel, both professionally and personally.

But JoJo is nothing if not resilient. Where many would have thrown in the towel, JoJo fought for her freedom. After years of legal battles, she finally emerged victorious in 2014, free from the shackles of her contract. This victory was not just about her ability to release new music—it was about reclaiming her voice and her sense of self. It was the beginning of a new chapter, one where JoJo would be in control of her narrative, both musically and personally.

Her comeback was marked by the release of *Mad Love* in 2016, an album that signaled JoJo's return to the spotlight but on her own terms. The album was a reflection of the pain, frustration, and resilience that had come to define the years she spent fighting to be heard. Tracks like "Fuck Apologies" demonstrated a new, unapologetic JoJo—one who was no longer afraid to speak her mind and own her truth. *Mad Love* received widespread critical acclaim and cemented JoJo's status as an artist who had not only survived the industry's worst but had emerged stronger.

JoJo's journey was far from over, though. In 2018, she took another bold step by re-recording her first two albums, *JoJo* and *The High Road*, under her own label, Clover Music. This move was symbolic of her reclamation of not just her music, but her identity. For years, her early works had been held hostage by her former label, but now JoJo had regained control. These re-recordings were not just a trip down memory lane—they were a powerful statement that JoJo owned her voice, and no one could take that away from her.

In addition to her career resurgence, JoJo also turned her focus inward, confronting the personal demons that had plagued her during her years in the industry. JoJo has been open about her struggles with mental health, body image, and addiction—issues that were exacerbated by the pressure to conform to the industry's unrealistic standards. But true to her resilient nature, JoJo has faced these challenges head-on, using her platform to advocate for mental health awareness and self-acceptance.

JoJo's willingness to share her vulnerabilities with the world has made her not just a pop star, but a beacon of hope for others who face similar struggles. She has become an advocate for self-care, urging her fans to prioritize their mental and emotional well-being. In doing so, JoJo has redefined what it means to be a successful artist. It's not about the number of records sold or the accolades received—it's about being true to oneself, even in the face of adversity.

Her return to Broadway in *Moulin Rouge!* in 2023 was yet another milestone in her career, showcasing her versatility as a performer. JoJo's ability to transition seamlessly from music to acting, while still maintaining her authenticity, speaks to her resilience and adaptability. This chapter of her career is not just a comeback; it is a testament to her ability to evolve and thrive, no matter the circumstances.

JoJo's legacy is one of perseverance. She could have allowed the industry to break her, but instead, she used her experiences as fuel to propel herself forward. Her journey is a powerful reminder that even in the darkest of times, there is always a way to rise again. For JoJo, the battles she faced—both internal and external—did not define her, but rather, they shaped her into the woman and artist she is today.

As she continues to release new music and take on new challenges, JoJo's story will undoubtedly inspire future generations of artists. Her unbreakable spirit, combined with her unwavering dedication to her craft, ensures that she will be remembered not just as a pop star, but as a symbol of strength, resilience, and triumph.